ALBATROSS

ALBATROSS

DORE KIESSELBACH

UNIVERSITY OF PITTSBURGH PRESS

Published by the University of Pittsburgh Press, Pittsburgh, Pa., 15260

Manufactured in the United States of America
Printed on acid-free paper
10 9 8 7 6 5 4 3 2 1

ISBN 13: 978-0-8229-6517-6
ISBN 10: 0-8229-6517-8

Cover photograph by Don Monroe
Cover design by Melissa Dias-Mandoly

For the responders

Errors are in the artist not the art.

–ISAAC NEWTON, PRINCIPIA

CONTENTS

LONGING

WINGS

PATHOLOGIST

On the way to the zoo we'd already seen
too often he said he needed to stop
and pick up some office paperwork.
In the hospital basement he walked
us to the cooler through the lab. We
passed pickled tissue, half-amphibians
gone wrong in glass jars. It was cold
behind those silver-handled doors,
shapes on gurneys, an orderly group
of four. Mom thought when we
told her that he'd used rights set
forth in their settlement to send
home a threat. And there were
times it seemed that he would kill
us. This time he only wanted us
to see where they would keep him
until the toxicology reports came
in and deformities in a heart with
enormous unmet needs and babies
who should never have been born.

DADA ONOMATOPOEIA

Your father asked about a movie you'd
seen, the kind parents used to drive
their children to at a local library
so they could continue the breakup
of their marriage alone. A character'd
leapt or fallen to his death. Again
and again he asked you whether
the dead one had gone *splat*. You
heard a word pulled so close
to being that it made no sense
of its own. It was unclear
then to science how some kinds
of squid reproduce. Over and
over you pretended not to
understand Dad's question
the way a biologist might
study a dream-like body
washed partly-decomposed
ashore and for reasons of his
own shake his head though,
after some uncertainty, he'd
found its point of origin.
It was a surfeit of barbiturates;
Dad did not go splat. You'd
been right not to say your answer.

BOB

was what his 7-11 nametag said. Part of his head
was missing. Tumor or crash, they'd excised
skull and left steel plate, thinner than bone,
behind. It made a dent where, if his
head were a hand, the fist would be.
When he couldn't find the right word,
he'd make a tapping motion there.
He let me eat without paying all
the chips I wanted from the rack.
It was a loneliness economy. Hours
a night for months, before I cycled
home to grim family dinners, we
leaned into one another behind the
counter as I flipped through his copy
of the paper I'd delivered. In time,
he trusted me alone with the cash
register. I learned to thwack coin
rolls on the counter's metal edge
and spill their silver innards in the
till. I never took a cent—even
rung up customers—though twice
or so, too embarrassed and young
to pay, I stuffed a *Hustler* down
my shirt. He saw that on a stock-
room monitor I didn't know about
but said nothing. Dad spoke louder
when he chose not to survive what
he'd lost. Like a piglet with an ape you
take your family where you can find it.

FALLOUT

I was sick at the fancy lunch after the judge took my name and gave me yours.
He'd looked hard at me before issuing the order. Perhaps he was clairvoyant
or the fever which flared up out of nowhere hours before the event had
made my eyes weirdly bright. No one else noticed anything. You thought
it would be a good time to make an effort, that lowering your guard at a
ceremonious moment would help us connect. As chilled forks were set
around us for a plate of iceberg hearts you told of an lieutenant in
charge of a military convoy who lost a nuclear warhead. In amber
waves of grain in the lead truck his driver, passing through them,
failed to notice the railroad crossing lights go on. The gate came
down behind him, and the drivers of the trucks that followed, each
laden with a lashed-down bomb, would have been jailed for trying
to beat the long freight train that split them from command and stopped.
Mixups about frequencies had created radio silence. When at last the
tracks were clear, truck three with its too-bright beacon of democracy
had gone looking for a bridge. *Lieutenant* means *placeholder* but there
would be no one else. I could have been a volunteer who spotted it for you.

OAK

I sat at it, a good table—one of a number
of respectable pieces they managed
to keep out of the weather until it lost
whatever appeal it had had for them,
until the disintegration of the marriage
gathered enough speed that they'd use
it, almost literally, as a barricade.
I'd been caught looking at nude
men in a *National Geographic.*
In fifth grade I knew how bad
the question was: *Are you homosexual?*
He was confused about the fact
that the older boys who raped him
when he was my age hadn't been
gay boys but psychopathic boys.
It took courage. It was the article
about the tribesmen who build
a forty-foot tree-limb scaffold
and tie a vine to it and to an ankle
and jump off face-first. Each ties
according to his height, weight,
sense of the materials, prevailing
winds, temperature, humidity, etc.
In the overall mass calculation
genitals matter little next to heads.
Because construction takes much

of the day, the last to go must
remember where the ground was.
His people will learn by torchlight
whether the vine stretched enough
to preserve the ball in its socket
joint, whether the tower gave
enough to place his lips on the earth.

WICKER MAN

after Robin Hardy's 1973 cult classic

In a low-slung sun, on a bluff overlooking an archi-
pelago, the 20-cubit eponym, by those who push
and pull the camera like a human sacrifice, is
dragged into view. Its wattle torso issues
curses voiced by this year's mainlander.
It wouldn't have happened to a conspiracy
theorist. A ringer for my stepdad, in a shiny
uniform, in a police boat, he arrived
pursuant to a reported disappearance
days before their solstice celebration.
The villagers could have surprised him
quayside and carted his cinctured body
straight to the place of burning but it
was required that he be given time to get
to know them. During his investigation,
he witnessed savage rites and found
them capable of a homicide that he
understood too late would be his own.
Stepping forward with a torch, their leader,
Mom in our family's improvised version,
reveals what now hardly requires it—the
child he meant to save had been a fiction.
Had he come to love it crops would grow.

ALIAS

People walk into propellers more often than
you'd think but mostly when distracted,
not with their eyes wide.
My brother tells the story.
It was a muni airport at night.
Several planes had landed
and a couple were about to leave.
It was loud where they'd gathered
and lit fluorescently.
The thing about fluorescence,
in context, is the beam:
it can strobe at multiples
of a propeller's spin.
Most of us have noticed
blades that seem to circle backward
slowly when we know
they're going forward fast.
But few will ever see
the stillness of pure harmony—
the logos of the maker
plain as day. My brother
finds the frequency.
My job is not to stray.

THE WEARER

NAUTILUS

The view from the duomo's roof's not to be missed.
Climbers and descenders in summer
fabric sweat's made less opaque
form helices of flesh that un-
twist flatly at the ends.
Those going up shoulder
a stone wall curving
as if for a boneless thing.
Those returning clamp
and slick the rail.
If you're up there, Lord,
and interested: give us
a spiral where the utmost
and the inmost points
are one. Daedalus used
an ant to draw a thread
through it. Some love
best the creature when it's gone.

OVERWINTERER

Dark spot on cardboard, when weather
kills those of your kind kept out
by the cinderblock I see you
on and off and when the cat who
joins me down the basement
stairs sees you I spare you
his investigation. I like your
company. Today I'm patient
till you stretch, learn there's tint
under your wings—a traffic-
cone monochrome for slowing
predators and speeding those
you give your ardent sounds.
The luscious wings painters
put on cherubs centuries ago
argue color is a way to paradise.
But you can risk no rhetoric—
no dragonfly clamps angels
in a vise. With an index
card and waterglass, I stressed
your predecessor when
the grass last greened;
I'll let you make your own
way out. If, instead, I find
you on a box of photos,

crisp and pale, I'll picture
insects finding me, slumped
unblinking in the yard,
ice-covered after summer hail.

HUNT AND PECK

The semi's aerial knocks a rising
thrush back down to roadside
shrubs it startled from. You hit
the brakes, pull over, ply the
green for breath, not half-
knowing what you're looking
for where grasses lean like
shadows from the earth.
Soon it's lusher than the
balance of the best life
left to you. Beyond road-
shoulder detritus you
find not a gouged eye
but the head that housed
it staring fiercely from
the other side. When
on the spot you teach
your hand a love dance
you can have it. Because
you're half-blind to what
you'd drag your own
feathers through you
bring it home. Be-
cause it's not a flight
risk you set it in the tub.

Offered cold-stunned
mealworms it won't
eat while you watch.
You stand in the hall
and listen, stand at first
that is, then sit, knees
pulled up to your chest.

HIT AND RUN

As if stepping sideways between two
close panes of glass I walked to him.
Stopped cars breathed like bulls
on the pavement.
Right there on the street
someone had torn him
a new one. Not really
looking for anything,
I looked into it.
Had I had the strength
to hold him to my eye
like a telescope I
would have seen nothing.
I'm sorry to say I would
have seen fragments
of skull, bone
porous as the cliff
palaces of the Anasazi.
He was conscious.
I spoke to him before
the police arrived.
The inside of your head
has unmatched beauty.

SHOP

Kept behind the counter is a list they bring to you.
You study it between a tarnished
tuba and the half-spun wingnuts
of an empty racquet press.
It's not a list they show to everyone.
It's the owner's private list,
the under-choreography
of a dance with customers
who know what they're
paying for and what with.
Some items have a single
buyer at their true price.
Eventually, he decided,
yours had none. You must
complete the purchase
to benefit from doubt.
But what you have in
mind has been marked down.

TREPHINATION

The procedure dates back millennia.
We open the skull and find a harp.
At first we think it's a folding knife.
To see what makes the harp
play we open the skull
wider and find a harpist,
without pants. At first
we think he wears red
pants. When a string
breaks, the harpist
composes something
willowy for the remaining
strings. That's versatility!
We don't worry about
hurting him; the brain
has no nerve endings,
connected as it
is to the absolute.
Like a child soldier, we
can ask him to do anything.

REPTILE

Fast-trundler, you move away from us until scrub parts,
know the instant you've become acres, pause there with
breathing eyes. Did you assume we'd skewer you
to the basking tree? There are such among our kind, it's
true. As for stopping where you do, barely subcutaneous
in the shade—do you fear what circulates deeper in
the undergrowth? Then close kin we are. There's this
branch of science that says you're in my head. When
gusts shake the juniper the scraps of blue are cursive you.

ROADKILL

In glare that hid more information than I thought had been lost
I guided deadly weight over a creature that didn't guess right.
An inch or two either way and I'm sipping coffee
and turning pages of my favorite magazine,
not having noticed anything in the mirror.
Its last slant leap was under, not away.
Stupid squirrel: tail rotoring, back legs
thrashing, forelegs flopping a bit.
It's head didn't move at all,
stuck to the ground by the brains.
How had I appeared to it?
More plain than a predator,
undazzled by the rodent waltz
of scurry, feint and dodge?
A turtle I thought to straddle,
skunks that stunk, name-
less things that came away
in parts. There have also been
some people subject to my art.

INSTALLATION

After Mr. Brown rewired his vacuum so that it blew down a duct-taped
nozzle and filled the cow lung, they jimmied the biology classroom lock
to steal it. It was the size of a too-full carry-on banished planeside to the hold.
No self-respecting teenager would have wrapped both arms
around it but I like to think they didn't use gloves as they carried
it dripping, crabwise across the empty quad, someone gripping
the remnant windpipe, others supporting it, slippery, from below.
The gentle Mr. McCann, our English teacher, taught that art
was made by people just a little more than we were like us.
That we could get there if we tried: a beautiful fable my good,
dead friend. Giving it footprints in my locker the artists tore a lobe.

DETERRENT

You buy the molded hippo legs, put them on,
then the back and headgear.
Hours later they haven't fused
and you're angry re the waste time.
Better spent doing a human,
you decide, which costs less
since you already own the parts.
Then linkages proliferate,
you mouth your hairless skin,
misconstrue and terrify
birds grooming your back.
Failing to relate well with the rest
of the herd proves you're not
a true amphibian. Water
infiltrates your tiny ears.
Once you toured a SAC base,
saw a superseded console,
its launch button never pushed.
How the hidden man had
yearned to stroke his clitoris.

EFFIGY

A laborer stands in the pay line on the bank of a broad river,
going unnoticed. The sun's been in his sweat all day
but is sinking now. He stands as shadows lengthen,
then touch the talk of those he worked with.
They speak of TV and alcohol and women
and when the shade encroaches they shiver
and the one in the midst of a story
about losing someone forever in a bar
forgets his place and is laughed at
by the others who call him Pa.
The laborer keeps to himself.
When handed his wages,
instead of walking with the others
to where the cars are parked
he enters woods beside the river.
His gait is that of someone
mending broken thoughts.
When he drops a slip of paper
your name's among the leaves.
Nothing's on your calendar.
Follow him through thickets
to the shelter he calls home.
Stand on ceremony.
Rise through old growth
that gnaws smoke like bone.

WORN

PLUME

Close upon a long hiccup in the light comes
clockwise torsion incident to the sound
of a huge cupped hand slapping water.
Concussion's shiver shuffles your guts
on its way to Tim's office and parts
northeast. Minutes later on the street
commuters flow up from the subway,
having heard—in clattering, reception-
less train cars—nothing. On a good
day it's horrible. Someone mentions
an airplane engine in the intersection.
Someone's had time to stretch yellow
tape. The professionalism of the
first response is outstanding but
you see how shocked the cops
are. North north north they chant
but keep turning back and looking
up. In a turbulent flow of faces
you recognize one, late to work,
not among the early birds lying
uncharacteristically down on the
job three blocks away. *What's going
on?* It's never been so hard to say.

ALBATROSS

Car bombs sound likelier to me than a burning
polygon. Today the Bridge, too, is a rumor.
Some of the thousands I'm on it with
bear residue of fire. On the far side
red, valve-sided trucks assemble.
I've told someone local I'm alive.
In the swelling cellular tsunami
forget outside the city. As part
of a long parenthesis I pass a lock-
jawed photographer athwart a large-
format camera on a platform. He
must have raced like a doctor here
with a bag so big he needed help
carrying it. I cede him my looking.
Tomorrow I'll see what he saw, on
the cover of the *Times*. I'm done
turning so learn later than most
that the blast heard in Brooklyn
mirrored a fall. There's no room
for takeoff here and it wouldn't be
right but someone crossed a wider
Channel on a bicycle with wings.
It was harder than he thought. Only
while maneuvering to board a water-
companion and give up the attempt
did he find the fluency he needed to go on.

BLOOD

Did you hear me? I was the one
shouting **donate blood**
on the streets of Brooklyn
as I ran from the Bridge
more than a mile for a
landline to my family.
The streets were crowded.
Many thousands
headed to Manhattan
hadn't gone, like
a colony of seabirds
on a cliff in a gale
were simply
trying to stay put,
thoughts of
feeding eclipsed
for the day. I was
a cliché: I had
to *do something*.
As if for the Barney's
sale we were
to stand in lines
in sum longer
than what had gone.
It was so busy
that I overflowed

and an attendant
came running.
Across boroughs
the impulse
rose like a tide.
But no moon
governed.
The harmed
had construed
enough of
sacrifice. In
our bloody
numbers
we were wrong.

DOWNWIND VACATION

paid for nothing (**smell**)
paid for nothing (smell)
paid for nothing (smell
paid for nothing (smel
paid for nothing (sme
paid for nothing (sm
paid for nothing (s
paid for nothing (
paid for nothing
paid for nothing)

WINDOWS ON THE WORLD

Looking for a black tie meant to hang straight,
I see the winged one with its clip I wore
at a law firm party atop the north tower,
that made the news for 20K spent
on roses flown from the equator.
It had been a banner year.
The last silk I held
I held against particulates
to my nose and mouth;
gram by gram it
more than dazzles
steel. The larva gets
a chance to boil *in*
situ without ruining
its cocoon. So high
above steerage, who
would have thought
to pray that nothing
should prevent us
from going down?
When the fog rolled
in like silk the city
shed its wings of light.
When the fog rolled
in like smoke we were
as good as drowned.

JACKS

After two weeks and an equinox we walk in wool
past men in camouflage with magazines and
one in a plastic suit waving then reading
from a wand. Blocks from buried fire
it burns where the pharynx and the voice
box meet. We're issued surgical masks
to wear inside the building. Ventilation
systems in the debris shadow spun pulver
in. An aerosol prayer that surrounds us,
spectacles, testicles, wallets and watches
dust timesheets that no one signed out of.
From a breakroom at the end of the hall
people dropping like jacks could be seen.
The game known to him as knucklebones,
Sophocles says, was invented at Troy—
something to keep the troops occupied
during fortnights of enforced idleness.
More light comes from that direction now.

GIRDER

I did touch it although you said no.
Bent and twisted it
was passing slowly
on a flatbed truck.
The trucks had been
emptying zero
around the clock
for weeks.
And would be.
You had wanted
to see it. Not like
one of the gawkers.
(They became
a kind of fringe,
like hair around
a body cavity.)
You thought
I would know
the best place
but I had made
it my business
not to know.
It was like searching
for a picnic spot
in a park full
of prospects.
It was a date.
I felt something.

CATAFALQUE

There are dragonflies in Manhattan
I learn when one uses me to rest.
I keep as still as I can, to be now
what I haven't been to any person,
a refuge, steady, reliable.
No one made me this way
any more than the sky makes
the dragonfly stagger when
a starling crosses overhead.
That's what I say to myself.
Were it to breathe fire on my finger
I would feel it as the pinch
of someone who wants
to believe he is dreaming.
Few of the boats driven
on the summer water
have carved dragonfly
prows, though wings
were oars on oars
before anything not
meant for water went there.

to the 9/11 tapes, the ones titled Brooklyn
Fire and Manhattan Fire and Manhattan
EMS, that last fifteen hours and contain
some of the most beautiful Americana
one could wish to encounter, set forth
in a context of historical authenticity.
Consider the early responder who
reveals that the first patients, from
flaming aviation fuel dropped down
elevator shafts, suffered terrible burns.
(Imagine those doors not opening.)
Soon after, as people commence
to defenestrate, he advises *be aware,
Manhattan, this is a hard hat operation,
a HARD HAT operation*. We hear
character holding up to strain, and
deep feeling. He is back on the city-
wide channel when Flight 175 hits.
On a leaking frequency someone
shouts **second plane**. A hand in-
voluntarily clutches the transmit
button. For several hundredths
of a second, firewalled engines
wail a thousand vertical feet away.

The next noise billows in rich
complexity past the physical limits
of its medium and is followed by
sounds of people breaking up.
When distinguishable voices rise
in many tones to the bare moment
we can still think there is hope for us.

CUT SHORT

CAULK

For who can be the herald, unless he have the voice of a Stentor?

Adjacent to a contractor's van, sawhorses stand outside the plant
where signs in Braille are made. At the wall behind the boss's
desk a man employs a gun for filling holes. A few houses
in the other direction, a neighbor continues to fly—
just below an American flag—a flag with an assault
weapon printed on it and the words *Come And Get It.*
It's too late for my generation to do so but (in God we trust)
one day one of the hundreds of children bused daily
past his barred windows, elected and stentorian, will.
Aside from the fact that our UPS driver—as always,
at the right place at the right time—was killed in passing
on the loading dock in his summer shorts, the facts
are repetition and the toll, seven, including the engraver
they were right to fire, about average. In his apartment
police found empty packaging for 12,000 rounds. What else
was the gun club, where he gave his muscles memory,
blind to? Or do they take instruction on how not to look?
As kids we groaned, hands held to wounds that hands
in the shape of a gun had inflicted, then got up again
savoring a darkness we'd concocted in ourselves.
We understood that we should be ready to lay our
lives down but none of us rehearsed for a factory floor.

FROZEN PLANET

Because I see it still I needn't see it
again—the exhausted wolf draped
on the exhausted ungulate, a two-
hour battle the documentary
had only a few minutes for.
The winter around them is
deep enough that they could
both die, depleted by the fight.
The *round* displays its basis
in the breaks they take,
panting side by side like
two tongues in the same
mouth. In the supplements
we learned that the camera-
man following from a chopper
the unphotographable larger
pursuit of the herd by a pack
had seen two take a tangent.
Playing a dowser's hunch
he chose where to set down,
skids scarcely touching the
snow as he hopped out miles
ahead of them with his gear.
In that ramified wild the odds
were against even a shot in
passing but they stopped

in the middle of his default
focus and gave us a long
and intimate conversation
about how difficult it is to
be on earth and how worth-
while. It's harder to look
at than the reflexive work
of the tabloid photographer
who saw someone pushed
to train tracks in front of him.
Many fewer of us have seen it.

ONE NATION UNDER

Pulled out and pronounced on the shoulder of the inter-
state, the plumber whose truck, alone at the time,
cartwheeled through the wide grass median,
launching elbow joints and crescent
wrenches isn't fully covered by the sheet
we drive past, because of flares and other
road irregularities, slowly. Steel-toed
work boots that will shield no more
protrude. Two expressionless troopers
await the county's corpse-transporting
van. Our license plates are eloquent:
vacation dwindled to its last hours, we're
headed for the border and the border
beyond that home from Yellowstone.
As I lean right to offer *sure is a shame*
through your down-rolled window one
draws with his foot in the dirt a line meaning
silence, that curves between us like a caldera's rim.

CONSIDERATION

The senior attorney and I had flown in
for a closing. Maybe it was the cadence.
The cabbie misheard us and dropped us
with a gesture in a direction he thought
was right. Why he'd have thought that,
with us in our silk and wool finery,
is anyone's guess. Sabotage, perhaps.
It's amazing how, half-bellwether,
half-wedge, the palaces of the rich
press upon poorer neighborhoods.
Though holding documents worth
millions we had nothing to worry
about. The homeless guy wanted
to help and knew where the Ritz
was. We would soon be standing
in belted terrycloth on marble. He
could have held our feet to the fire
but closed with us *pro se* for change.

FIRED

I've read that in some places firing
someone's an elaborate process
designed to minimize actual
confrontation. No one wants
to gain the face that's lost so
hints are given. If picked up
on soon enough, these allow
leaves to fall gracefully from
a tree. Sometimes, bosses
must gently shake a branch.
And perhaps, then, even
less gently. Deeper in
the article we meet a poor
soul deemed redundant in
hard times, whose fate
fell to an electrician
whose job it daily was
to attenuate the flow
of current to the worker's
light, a subtle diminishment
sure to go unnoticed at first.
How soon, for example,
after it began to fail,
did you discern the fridge
was getting warm?

And to test your hypo-
thesis didn't you press
the back of your hand
to some bacon
as if to the forehead
of a coughing child?

RENDITION

When there is consensus they unlock the box
and find a pair of silver hands, crafted
as though by Dürer, inventor of hands.
An index finger tapers to a removable
nail on the underside of which, when light
is held just so, a graven word
appears. The first of them to say
it finds a feather on his tongue.
As they articulate each digit
the darkness grows no orifice
they can widen with their ears.
Blaming faulty intel they decide
it's time to go, but the hands reach
up from the box so it can't be closed.

CRUCIFIXION

One minute he's looking at you, full-size, in anguish,
and the next he's a stricken Harryhausen figurine.
Someone with cooler blood would be wishing
for a compendium of diseases but you're
pressed too personally into the event
to separate symptoms from suffering.
If it can be thought to do so, horror
flows like gas from an unlit oven,
well past the point where it makes
any sense at all to strike a match.
When he says *there's this awful*
pounding in my head no one has
the heart to tell him *it's not in your head.*

ASSYRIAN FRIEZE

The good society's shown in forty yards of carving
stripped from foreign walls. The fisherman
faces fish in such a way that they can be said
to be equal. Grain grows straight under a stone
sun. Parading through the capitol, castes
and classes appear to have found dharma.
Tendons rise as grace notes in horse legs.
Patterns in fabric worn by onlookers
on the far side of the avenue appear
through the wheels of passing carts—
squares with centered dots inscribed
like hearts. Left to right the story
flows, until this panel holds you.
Though you'd reached it in reverse,
the meaning of the place where
people are quieted by blades
would have been conveyed
in clear, contemporary logic.
Beyond the city, warriors have
assured continuing prosperity,
among hirers of artisans at least.
Within—swords being already
out for captured remnants of the
other side's army—citizens who
failed to line up in time or who
otherwise no longer conform are

being trimmed from the picture.
Because with each blood drop the
heads grow heavier they're carried off
by locks twisted twice around wrists.
Leaning in as if to locate something
you hear a docent say that music is
depicted only in the place of execution.

MIGNON

I'll never have a better steak though the meat
could be more tender and my back alley
view of the Acropolis less obscured.
That it cost three bucks and came with
crisp fries by the scad and a chipped
carafe of local wine further predisposes
me to forgive the Greeks for letting
their civilization fall to pieces.
Caraway seeds of destruction were
present, I've read, in the pillared
shrine. Between real and seeming
symmetry, they skewed the lines
for their eyes, not hers for whom
they once had named themselves,
optical refinements, the experts
say: 70,000 noninterchangeable
parts and hardly a right angle in
the place. My favorite distortion
would have irked her most—*entasis*,
the bulging in the column meant to
show it, like a muscle, bearing weight.

MONARCH

For helping a judge empty his office I'm rewarded
with a cap on which an eagle clutching arrows
spreads the golden wings of Washington's authority.
I bear no federal power, but on summer rides
acquire a taste for doubletakes, flinches and nods
that come without any pretense on my part,
I tell myself, mounting up for spins through
noticing citizens. A September festival cele-
brates the butterfly that through my northern
city also dawdles, lolls and zooms. Science
displays, puppet shows, wide drums, and dancers
in feathery, pre-Colombian regalia
intermarry cultures that an insect connects.
We make a Sunday of it, belly up to a food
stand selling Mexi-Corn—roasted sweet
corn drenched in butter and cream then
sprinkled with crumbly cheese. It's delicious
my wife will agree, after making room
for me on a wooden bench facing
spirited interpretations of Toltec and Maya.
The brown-skinned proprietor turns
and gives a sign to a man behind him
who's missing some teeth, who reaches
into a roaster that has simplified his
hand while aging it. Two young men
chopping onions and peppers at a counter

have slowed, wary, watchful. When
from the main stage a horn sounds
four times—long, clear and sweet—
the ache of migration is in the sound
but it's not plaintive, not in any way.
While filling a paper boat with melted
fat for my ear the man stops and asks
if I know why they do that. I answer
without thinking much. In inflected
English he says no, it's the directions,
if you don't forget them you can get
back again. And he glances skyward
as his ancestors might have while
mine were inventing pollution. I say
yes, it's very beautiful, I've taken
lots of pictures. My change is five times
what the item cost and twice what I paid.
When my beak closes I have lost the way.

FRONTIER

Peeling an orange a man sees a toothpick poking through tight segments.
Carefully unstringing pith, he finds the top spars and crow's nest
of a little mast, complete with rigging, deep in pulp. At last the delicate
surgery begins, he says to himself, bringing the orange to a room
where instruments for dissecting citrus glint the walls.
Working laparoscopically with saws as small as seeds,
he clears a fresh-swabbed deck, coiled rope, gunwales,
keel, wheel, rudder, compass and log. And underneath
the tiny ship a rind-cupped, orange sea. He lays the whole
hull bare and no less gingerly than if it were a cherry
bomb extracts the vessel with its flea-sized crew.
Studying the phenomenon through a sticky loupe,
he sees sailors with undone hopes of destination
rise and be subdued. *They might as well be aliens,*
he remarks in a note as, rote as theme park actors
after a double shift, they walk a plank that was never
more than a splinter holding things upright in a new world.

CAMPESINO

He found himself in trouble in Guatemala in days
of disappearance, death squads and rumors of organ theft.
In the town where he was staying a bus station
served as the seat of government.
They brought him there to view the *gringa*
killed on the path to the volcano. She was lying
on a table beneath chalk departure times.
Were brain transplants possible, hers, perforated
front to back behind the proverbially neat
hole, wouldn't have been worth much.
He told me this story thirty years
ago, one of those self-annealing,
incidental conversations that attach
themselves like license plates to a life.
His parents had died, leaving him enough
money to circle the globe, roughly, once.
(He was on a bus in India that rolled wheels-
over-roof down a mountain, killing
half on board; to extricate himself,
he did something, unmentionable
to this day, crawling through the glass.)
Rumor had it he was a black belt
but when they came for him later,
carrying knives and their fathers' guns,
he spoke a Spanish he didn't know
he knew and when he faltered someone
in homespun behind him spoke for him.

THE BIRTH OF THE SYLLABLE

You said I should write about the fact that I'm coming to the end
of a Maya 52-year cycle. I'm not connected by blood or memory
to that story-drenched culture but it does populate me at the
idea level, like spray at the top of a fizzy drink. During more
than a century, some of the world's loneliest and most gifted
people made it comprehensible enough to us that I think
I understand what the countdown period in the cycle is for.
The graphical unit of sense was a square that first contained
a single eye-word. I'm getting it wrong but cultural pressure
over time forced several logograms into the same quadrilateral.
Integrating them was an art passed down person to person
within a scribe caste that exists today, switched to phonemes
by those friars who didn't for their love of pictures kill them.
Long absent from the scriptoriums of Seville, that echoing
calligraphy lives in the hands of indigenous people who can
neither read nor write except in the stolen tongue of Christ.
They already know the world didn't end as it was meant to.

LONGING

DISAPPEARANCE

The tide comes in like an old house.
It is where you would have lived.
Darkness is in its joints and its
shingles clack. It slumps over,
reaching shore. You study it
alone. The one you came here
with is gone. Sunlight had
been vanishing when you
saw her last, gathering from
among stones she found
at the tide line the ones
she liked best. She filled
her pockets with them.
As the light lengthened
and lowered it found parts
of her body that you had
not thought would pass light.

AULOS

an ancient Greek wind instrument that accompanied choral singing

Was it the guidebook or did you see it in passing and say stop?
We were headed south, for Sparta, but pulled the car
over, walked down into it, looked back at grass-softened
layers of stone from the direction the actors would have.
Our faces were petals pushed by the wind. For what earthly
purpose did we seek another countenance. Or was it only
I? Greece had been my vote for the best way to spend
your windfall trip fund. I'd been reading Herodotus
in our roachy residential hotel when the letter arrived.
Would knowing they applied bright paint to the Parthenon
have changed our destination? You were interested in where
the audience would have looked when the action turned
their eyes away. With terraces they made farms of hills,
shoulder upon shoulder holding the sky up like a flaming
bier. In the tiny top plot it was customary to plant a flowering
tree and water it religiously when the crops failed, which
we forgot to do or which ate shit on my shift. I claim
nothing of the scenes that followed save a blade of grass.
By thumbs held out of character it could have been a reed.

PELOPONNESUS

Two weeks revolved in prospect like a postcard stand.
Your mother's money'd gotten us a clean room
near a school. She hadn't much but meant
to help us build from scratch a world.
Would we have dropped out sooner had we known?
Wakened from a lovers' nap by tidal choruses
of play rising through the wide window,
we lay, drowsy, murmuring plans for the islands
through young life's yelled elation and alarm.
We didn't know that Pelops was the eaten
Isaac of an older god, hadn't learned the bed
is a soft fulcrum between kinds of sacrifice.
Broken marble still to come, speechlessness
not yet a bandage we couldn't stop picking at,
those unscratched minutes were our golden age.

CENOTE

It's what I think of when I think of trying to explain myself to your sacrifice,
office days spent in worsted so that I may wear a wetsuit in limestone
caverns in the Yucatan full of captured rain unstirred for centuries.
We shared one once, when we breathed underwater side by side.
Island ferry to a bus to a jungle pool a hillside had made room
for. Like syllables we entered that dark mouth backward,
unsaying ourselves in zero turbidity, a clarity wasted in
darkness so total that it blinds and makes translucent
all that live there. With the flashlight on, it's entering a mirror,
but it's not oneself one sees. The beam sweeps like resolution
two thousand feet. One follows it. Yes, there have been sacrifices here.

PLAYING POSSUM

A scream evolved to scrape DNA, low to the ground
and right against the foundation. You know
you should investigate but sink sleepward
under a third attempt to untangle the warm
bedclothes. When snow retreats to shadowy
parts of the yard, you'll find one of North
America's only marsupials turned inside-out
at the top of its range. Not hibernators, they
unkink themselves from culverts and come
looking for a meal. Placing the spine in a plastic
bag, you'll recall its encounter with another
of its kind last winter at the compost bin.
Wound-up unseeing in themselves they
advanced from opposite corners of the yard
toward icy eggshells and rigid coffee grounds.
When their noses touched each fell over
backward dead to the world. It was no act.
Through binoculars you could see it as clearly
as if it were happening in your own house.

MAGINOT

After consecutive eons the moon succeeds
in drawing another kind of gaze from us.
Nothing steers by it, nothing is coming home.
Like the cirrus around its globe of light
we can drift away from an old dividing
line. At important moments *la patrie*
wanted one working phone connected
to divisions in the field. It was a nation
as predisposed to messengers as I am
to the women who interrupt us now.
Expecting solitude on their own late
walk, they've seen us on the park
bench and hesitate, not sure they're
not our reason for being here. What
do the statistics say? Were I to ring
them and explain that we're no one's
reason for being here my voice would
travel a great distance though they're
closer than I once could throw a ball.

SPACEWALK

The heavy lifting's already been done elsewhere by others.
They go out, they come in, what could be simpler?
But the handle on the hatch won't work. A spring
intended to release a deep mechanical clasp isn't.
So there Jim McDivitt and Ed White are—not
the first Americans to visit space but the first
meant to exit their closet-sized capsule
there (try ninety-eight hours cooped in
one of those)—with a *Gemini* mission
on the line and a Cold-War-anxious nation
tuned in. When the glitch had happened
in a run-through at Canaveral, McDivitt,
watched a ground crew take the lock
assembly's gears apart. But a single
loose-screw moment here means
nobody's coming home. In the un-
gainly gloves he might as well perform
deconjoinment surgery on his fellow-
traveler. It can't be an order, will
barely make the news. White makes
himself as small as possible during
the dismantlement then scoots past
his colleague to take the longest walk
ever, off the shortest pier. (He'll burn
alive when *Apollo*'s door won't open
on a launch pad in how many years?)

Falling free, he sets aside thoughts of
whether their vehicle can be made air-
tight for reentry to describe in audible
ecstasy an oscillant point of light on
Earth's adrift horizon that, in seconds,
becomes more light—*whoa!*—than any
friendly eye has seen before. Addressing
the descriptive burden of a panoramic sun-
rise viewed from space, he corrects himself
twice. As radiance crowns the world's blue curve
really something becomes *tremendous* then *just beautiful.*

WINTER DOCUMENTARY

Property law says we own a column of air
above our house to the edge of space,
but we're too cozy to claim anything
beyond the chimney and a satellite
dish tonight. As in the flickering
hearth windfallen limbs draw
oxygen, a former astronaut
recalls a dream he had while
tucked in his foil berth on the
moon. Bounding in the lunar
rover he spotted tracks leading
away from the landing site
in a direction by NASA un-
explored. Putting pedal to
metal through an airtight
sole he rolled past night
mares of Tranquility and
Clouds. When Mission
Control had a problem he
toggled the comm switch
off. Earth dangled upside
down like a spigot over-
head as he stopped be-
hind a doppelgänger vehicle
that had idled there for
eons, pits in its chassis

told. Wiping dust from
the visor of its recumbent
occupant he found his
own face staring back
at him, marooned in
the journey's mirror.
It rattled him, realizing
that he'd seen it all before.
Drawn less these days
to distance we turn the tele-
vision off. Moonlight
finds us under its own
power and melts in the fire's glow.

JANUARY KITE FESTIVAL

Over banners augered in yard-thick lake ice, a bounding galleon
casts a shadow EKG on snow. Nylon dragonflies zip below
a six-foot lemon inchworm heedless of a grape carp
watching it unfold. Toting steaming cups of coffee,
untethered parents congregate while everywhichway
children squeal like kits outside the den. On a walk
to reverse inwardness we've found the sky's tail
where fish scales have been. When our eyes give
back the motion they've lifted from our mouths
we pledge to raise our own string in the coming year.
Beneath a butterfly you send away for, that takes
all we can unroll for it, it's a promise we honor and keep.

NORTHERN CONSERVATORY

In winter clothes in green-
house heat, we form a slow
line between the upward
ambience of Neem
trees and the readiness
of ladyslippers for
a winged foot. Snow
visible through beaded
streaks in arching
glass would refresh
us now but the spice
trees ahead are worth
sweating longer for.
Giant ferns and trees
of paradise and
mosses and wild
coffee from the
Amazon also breathe
in the sunstruck
room. The older
couple resting
on a bench came
for that respiration.
She's the leader,
the shoot that
shows the way.

She rises and sets
her hips and hoists
him upright with a
sudden potent pull.
Standing and being
stood is love in this
late and early season.
When the practiced
isometric act occurs
time comes and goes,
fluid in an upright vein.

HUMMINGBIRD

We saw eight or nine and heard others
unzipping air above us. Lolling purple
thickets in the hilltop public garden
drew them. One returned from
darting sorties to the blossoms
nearest us. Sunlight glazed the
rapier of its outthrust tongue.
It pushed bees back with wing-
wind as it drank then withdrew
from a nectared sheath to parry
shining onslaughts of its own kind.

BURIAL

The housecall-making hospice vet you looked at in-
differently at first, then in anger when she needled
you in loose skin between your shoulder blades,
then not at all—because we'd turned you to face
late afternoon light in the trees—has come
and gone. Yesterday's rain made the clay
below the flat stone you loved to bask
on even clayier, but having seen you cope
with organ failure I'm not going to short
change you on depth. Unlike in a movie,
your eyelids haven't proved easy to close—
you look on unblinking from the patio
as I strain for a spacious cavity of earth.
Then on your fleece I lay you in it. Then
she (a whole other direction of love,
as you knew) and I cover you with
cloth and tokens of our time together
then catnip from your favorite patch.
Rolling in the midst of it you asked us
with eyes that had deepened and grown
reptilian whether we understood how
beautiful it all was, a centered look
of pleasure so absolute that we who
bought your death had lost it. As
light departs the high limbs we hold
emptiness between us in a lingering

embrace. She crumbles clay over
you with her hands, that the first
layers not be lumpen, then goes in
to make dinner. After shoveling
and tamping and shoveling and re-
placing that old river rock, with you
on the other side now, I follow her in.

NOTES

— "Alias": The referenced optical illusion, by which pulsing light may cause a rotating object to appear stationary, is called aliasing or the wagon-wheel effect.

— "Deterrent": The Strategic Air Command, or SAC, was "responsible for Cold War command and control of two of the three components of the U.S. military's strategic nuclear strike forces" (Wikipedia).

— "Plume," *et seq.*: I worked for the New York City Housing Authority, three blocks northeast of the World Trade Center site, on the morning of September 11, 2001.

—"Albatross": On June 12, 1979, pilot and cyclist Bryan Allen crossed the English Channel in a seventy-pound, human-powered aircraft designed by Dr. Paul MacCready, named *Gossamer Albatross*. It is pictured mid-journey on the cover of this book.

—"Blood": Barneys is an upscale clothier in New York City favored by lawyers and other white-collar professionals. Its annual half-off sale produces long and anxious lines.

—"Windows on the World" was a restaurant facility, with a venue for corporate events, located in World Trade Center 1 (north tower).

—"Caulk" is for Keith Basinski, *in memoriam.*

— "Frozen Planet" is the title of a BBC nature documentary series.

—"Consideration": *Pro se* is a Latin term meaning "on one's own behalf." It is applied to parties in a legal proceeding who are not represented by counsel.

—"Rendition," or "extraordinary rendition" is a practice of the United States government involving the seizure and transport of persons to secret foreign locations for unconstitutional, "enhanced" interrogation.

—"Maginot": The Maginot Line "was a line of concrete fortifications, obstacles and weapon installations that France constructed . . . during the 1930s. . . . French military experts extolled [it] as a work of genius, believing it would prevent any further invasions from the east." (Wikipedia).

ACKNOWLEDGMENTS

Grateful acknowledgement is made to the editors of magazines and anthologies in which the following work first appeared (sometimes in earlier forms and under different titles):

5 AM: "Fired"; *AGNI*: "Alias," "Catafalque," "Winter Documentary"; *Ascent*: "Caulk," "Peloponnesus"; *Cortland Review*: "Plume"; *diode*: "Bob," "Maginot"; *FIELD*: "Disappearance"; *Freshwater Review*: "Consideration"; *Green Mountains Review*: "Dada Onomatopoeia"; *Magma (UK)*: "Campesino"; *Malahat Review*: "Frontier," "Nautilus"; *Manchester Review (UK)*: "Assyrian Frieze," "The Birth of the Syllable," "Monarch"; *Midway Journal*: "Hunt and Peck," "Playing Possum"; *Miramar*: "Spacewalk"; *New Orleans Review*: "Pathologist"; *Phoebe*: "Deterrent"; *Pleiades*: "Girder"; *Plume*: "Albatross," "Crucifixion," "Downwind Vacation," "I'm Listening Again," "Installation," "Oak"; *Plume 3 Anthology*: "Windows on the World"; *Plume 4 Anthology*: "Aulos"; *Poetry City USA, Vol. 4*: "Roadkill"; *Poetry Review (UK)*: "Frozen Planet"; *Portland Review*: "Rendition"; *Rattle*: "Mignon"; *Red Wheelbarrow*: "January Kite Festival, " "Overwinterer"; *The Rialto (UK)*: "One Nation Under," "Trephination"; *Sonora Review*: "Reptile"; *Sleet*: "Jacks"; *Stand (UK)*: "Blood," "Hit and Run," "Shop"; *Water~Stone Review*: "Effigy."

"Caulk" also appeared, with original artwork by Susan Solomon, in a limited edition broadside from Red Bird Chapbooks. "Consideration" also appeared in *Minnesota Litigator* under the title "Junior Attorney." "Girder" also appeared in *It Starts with Hope* (Nodin Press, 2016), an anthology of writing and images donated to the Center for Victims of Torture. The third section of this book first appeared as a group in the online magazine *Plume*, together with an introduction and notes about my personal experience of 9/11 and of the obstacles I encountered writing about it.

Deepest thanks to the Minnesota State Arts Board and the citizens and taxpayers of Minnesota for funding that was essential to the completion of this work; to Joan Larkin, Anne Marie Macari, Katrina Vandenberg, and David Young for their generous support when needed most; to Stuart Friebert and Daniel Lawless for life-changing friendship, literary and beyond; to Ed Ochester for space in the sparkling Pitt Poetry Series; and to fellow Pitt Poetry Series authors for cultivating an incomparable readership over fifty years.

By virtue of her inspiration, sympathy and leadership my wife Karin Ciano is a full collaborative partner in anything that is right about this book.